My treasure trove of emotions

Bindu Unnikrishnan

BookLeaf Publishing

India | USA | UK

Presentation by *BookLeaf Publishing*

Web: www.bookleafpub.com

E-mail: info@bookleafpub.com

ISBN:9789360940195

First edition 2024

DEDICATION

To the strong and beautiful women who dare to dream,

This book is dedicated to you, the fearless souls who dare to defy boundaries, challenge norms, and reach for the stars. You are the embodiment of strength, resilience, and grace, inspiring others with your courage and determination.

May the words within these pages serve as a beacon of empowerment, reminding you of your limitless potential and the boundless possibilities that await you. May you continue to dream boldly, chase your aspirations relentlessly, and carve your own path with unwavering confidence.

In a world that often seeks to confine and define, you stand tall as a testament to the power of dreams and the beauty of resilience. Here's to you, the architects of your destiny, the warriors of hope, and the eternal dreamers!

With admiration and gratitude,

Bindu Unnikrishnan

ACKNOWLEDGEMENTS

To my beloved daughter, Tanisha, whose enduring affection and insatiable curiosity illuminate the world's wonders. She has been my guiding beacon, offering unwavering support, motivation, and faith in my aspirations. While my husband remained quietly supportive, his constructive criticism was a valuable contribution. Keeping pace with me was a challenge he graciously accepted.

I extend profound gratitude to my parents whose love, counsel, and sacrifices have shaped my character. Deep appreciation for my sister, Deepa, for her steadfast belief in me and for nurturing my creative spirit.

To my treasured friends who stood by me through every twist and turn of this journey, your companionship is a priceless treasure. Special thanks to those who urged me to pursue my passion for poetry, providing the encouragement I needed to spread my wings.

Lastly, to those who whispered, "What if you fly, honey?"—your simple query ignited a fire within me, prompting me to embrace the unknown and strive for greatness. Your unwavering belief in me empowered me to surpass even my loftiest aspirations.

With sincere gratitude,
Bindu Unnikrishnan

PREFACE

In the tapestry of human experience, emotions are the threads that weave intricate patterns across the canvas of our lives. "My treasure trove of emotions" is a collection that captures the essence of these emotions, delicately crafted into pearls of poetry.

As the reader embarks on this journey through the pages of this book, they are invited to explore the depths of human feeling—from the gentle warmth of a smile to the poignant ache of whispered confessions, from the raw intensity of pain to the exuberant dance of joy. Each poem within these pages is a window into the kaleidoscope of emotions that color our existence, inviting reflection, empathy, and understanding.

With every turn of the page, the reader is drawn deeper into a world where beauty and heartache coexist, where moments of lightness are intertwined with shadows. Through lyrical verses and evocative imagery, the poet invites us to pause, feel, and connect with the shared humanity that unites us all.

"My treasure trove of emotions" is not merely a collection of poems; it is a journey—a journey through the labyrinth of emotions that define our human experience. It is a testament to the power of words to touch the soul, to heal, and to illuminate the beauty that resides within the depths of our hearts.

May this collection serve as a companion to those navigating the complexities of their own emotions, offering solace, inspiration, and a reminder that within the depths of vulnerability lies the essence of our strength.

My dream, my story!

Not to rewrite stories of old,
But to create new ones, bold.
Not to drift, but to take control,
Shaping my own destiny, whole.

I chose myself when tiredness loomed,
Refusing to be swallowed, or consumed.
This time, I won't sink low,
I've learned to float, to rise, and grow.

Though worn, I'm not shattered,
Determined, my spirit unfractured.
With faith in myself, unshaken,
I'll weave words yet unspoken.

My voice will ripple, my words will fly,
Encouraging others to reach for the sky.
This won't be just another tale spun,
But the story of my dreams, begun.

Diva adorning the crown

Conquest for some, isn't coincidental
toiling through is their mantra,
hence they are mighty inspirational.

Resilient and compassionate,
their reasons and causes are very passionate.
Dreamers and hard workers are they,
who create their path in even unpaved ways

They lead the path, spreading their light
their invisible crown shines
with their aura and insight

To my valentine

Not the prettiest of red roses,
 but the gaze, that acknowledges my bloom,
not another dinner out, with candles,
 but a nod, when I prepare my healthy legumes.
Not another stroll hand in hand,
let's work together and clean our land,
no world economy, sitting on the couch,
 but let's discuss our future plans.

Let us plant a tree, play with dirt,
and tell the world about things we care
Let us fix that broken window pane,
maybe the cold tonight will be easy to bear
No movies, plays, or recitals I need,
hear out today my little prayer
Counting our blessings let us make a pact,
Triumph together, and together we shall fall.

No chocolate or fancy wine I shall need,
but the time to hear our little one's mischief
maybe a round of cards, we shall play,
remembering how we met and continued to stay.
The game of counting stars in the sky,
 holding hands we feel the grass beneath
maybe I shall tell you then, my favorite color,

and where I strive to reach.

The valentine song

Swiftly through the wind
When you sent whispers
It was then, that my heart
 Just skipped a beat
for it reminded millions of moments
that I imagined, but couldn't live

the promises to meet,
ended in retreat
for parallel, we flow
like those river banks that never meet.

Like the fragrance of the garden blooms
May you live without any gloom
May this valentine, like every other,
Wishes, not rose petals make their way to you.

The language of love

This Valentine is just sunshine
For the warmth that can wither the snow
The soft wind and chimes
reminds me that from miles
Your deeds are what make heavens know

Make that little puddle for birds
Where they quench their thirst after the day
Little food shared with stray
Let them feel that we didn't leave them astray

A hug of blankets perhaps to the homeless
a special meal for orphans too
Your little deeds of kindness
Is how your love speaks through!!

A warm little meal with your near ones
sharing dreams with your best friend
Little dance barefoot on grass alone
With stars staring down admiring your light and
glow.
What makes Valentine so special
is the love inside you, coming through,
spreading warmth and kindness
Even gods in heaven will smile at you.

Green with Envy

It isn't about the green cover
not about my plants or trees
'green with envy ' is what I mean
when I dance to my success and scream about
my dreams.

Trust and strength is what one hope
to blow my trumpet with your mighty force
Where is the scope for envy then,
when a friend is with whom you bare your soul,
now and then.

When you showed my scars and laughed at my
whims,
I started dreaming about how to challenge it, and
might as well win

I love to play hard and dance to my tune
For my every win, I know you will cringe.

Dream of a woman

In the garden of her imagination, colors dance,
Vibrant shades adorn her dreams, a captivating
trance.
She holds within her, a treasury of countless
dreams,
Nestled deep within her, like treasures in hidden
streams.

Each dream a jewel kept safe in her heart's
embrace,
A tapestry of hues, bringing her solace and
grace.
Not a dull moment in sight, her dreams abound,
In her secret sanctuary, they quietly astound.

Her dreams, a vibrant mosaic, never dull or
plain,
They flourish within her, like a colorful refrain.
In this private haven, they thrive and bloom,
Nourishing her spirit, dispelling all gloom.

With each dream, a story untold,
In their symphony, her spirit unfolds.
A vision that illuminates her darkest night,
Guiding her path with its radiant light.

So let her dreams blossom, let them soar,
For in their brilliance, she finds so much more.
A woman of courage, strength, and grace,
In her vivid dreams, she finds her rightful place.

The rear-view mirror

The eyes that caught mine
through the rear-view mirror
had dreams bubbling,
like the meandering river
that had plans of never settling.

The smile that wasn't visible
due to the smallness of the mirror,
reflected through the lines that appeared
between those eyes and that ear.
It set the cord of my heart with pulsating beats
which resonated with my thumping heartbeats.

I knew love had arrived without any notice
It swept me off my feet and left me restless a bit.
For any societal rules were unknown to my heart
 that was set to dance to his mysterious beats.

Swiftly the sails adrift, the voyage took a turn
 which even the winds didn't notice a bit,
When can one control the heart
that had set to dance to all his mischief

When the windows rolled down
came the gush of fresh wind

that flew my hair and
dangled my earrings
The eyes in the mirror still caught it right
for when did it ever leave the sight.
It held my gaze and I noticed that glint
I knew love had arrived without a hint.

For the eyes shrunk again
this time to acknowledge my blushing smile
It answered the unspoken question left unsaid in
a long while.
Enamored beyond any restrain
I knew my heart had given away
and it turned itself to a hearty laugh.

Memories of Rains

The scent of rain, with you by my side,
Seeking shelter, a playful bet we tried.
Nothing escaped the drenching wet,
Eyes, body, and soul, all in unrest.

Climbing the slippery slope, memories not so
sweet,
Recalling touches in the rain, our bodies in heat.
Breath held tight, cherishing each clutch,
Entwined for hours, a passionate touch.

Cracks in the universe, moments rare and new,
Time paused, senseless, the stillness grew.
Sky trembled with thunder's cry,
Clouds waged war, chaos in the sky.

Our breath intertwined, a rhythm divine,
As time danced, tender touches aligned.
Like celestial lights in evening's hue,
Rain's nostalgia stirs memories anew.

A million moments lived and loved,
In the sky's embrace, memories rise above.

The stranger in the house

When you didn't know the story
yet reacted with gory,
I knew that a stranger had come into the house.

The one who knew me well
yet didn't know how to tell
I knew that the stranger had messed up my head.

The waging war by tongues alone
For causes still clearly unknown,
I knew the control the stranger had asserted all
along.

To overthrow and derail
so that the mighty ego shall prevail,
I knew that the stranger had geared up pretty
well.

When the choices were made separate
And the decisions were made in haste,
I knew the invisible wall building up across the
hall.

Blame assigned, promises stagnant,

The stranger's true nature is transparent and
adamant.
No anticipation of change, the truth remains,
In the stranger's realm, I endured the strains.

Imperfectly Perfect

From birth, I stood out with a form incomplete,
A cocoon's embrace torn, leaving me replete.
Though the time for perfection slipped away,
I emerged complete, without delay.

My growth revealed a crude and alien sight,
My form distinct, a puzzling blight.
Unlike my kin, my wings refused to soar,
The dream of flight seemed forevermore.

Tender care and unwavering support,
Yet my wings remained stubbornly short.
Their patterns mismatched, a discordant hue,
A stark contrast to the beauty I knew.

Their vibrant hues and intricate designs,
Mine dull and plain, causing endless lines.
Ugly I felt, unworthy of their grace,
My isolation, a bitter embrace.

Amidst my despair, a butterfly took flight,
Adorned in colors that filled me with delight.
"Your wings," it said, "a perfect disguise,
Concealing you from predators in the skies."

Not flying high, a unique and precious gift,
Protecting you from danger's swift drift.
You are rare, I was told, one in a million,
An exceptional creation, a perfect specimen.

With newfound confidence, I pondered its claim,
The imperfect me, multi-faceted and grand.
Just then, a trap appeared, a sinister snare,
A colorful spectacle of wings beyond compare.

Into its depths, they flew, their brilliance bright,
But I, with my leaf-like wings, remained out of
sight.
My inability to soar proved my escape from
death,
For the trap's deceit I saved myself.

In my imperfection, I found my true worth,
A design unique, a rare gift to unearth.

The stretched mind

The harder I fell, the higher my bounce
problems still gnawing, but I tossed it to trounce
No enemy pulled me down,
Those were the deceitful near ones,
who mercilessly broke me down.
The faces were many, hard to narrow down,
but their actions were the same, relentlessly
grind me to dust.
Swords of tongue or the hostile glare
restless it left me, in numerous accounts
Tasteless arguments, bitter blows
Every word was a weapon to knock me down.
Into the shell, I pushed myself,
to escape the mysterious hell
The pain and life conjoined as one
made me the labeled one.
Selfish they called me,
who revel within oneself
In my pursuits and my loneliness
I created heaven and hell.
The mind that is stretched
far beyond its elastic limits
Is never bound to go back
and check it's spirits
For consistently it flows

my ideas that heaven beholds
To rest in peace the voices
which tells me to slow and bend below.

Sound of success

Deafening loud, resounding beats
to the enemy, it pricks, like a million needles
beneath.
Thumping the ground the victorious rise
the roar trembling the clouds in the sky.

Wounded, yet calm, and resolute
the bells of victory chime in his pursuits
He doesn't detest on anyone's behest
Claims goodwill and constantly marches his
best.

Uncountable days and nights he worked,
He works through distractions, seeking no rest
When the whole world sleeps soundly and
dream
He slogs and runs without a scream.

Is his success just a fluke,
Is it noise when he plays his solo flute
The sound of success plays the tune
those working hard can resonate, and croon.

Boundless Love

Who said love needs a relationship
It's free to give, free to feel
When tied,it suffocates to death,
when left free, blooms like wealth

A word cant define, a million emotions
A gaze held says more than, words of devotion
Love crosses boundaries, seldom withheld
Like wind it flows, does it stop when held?

Confuse not, duty with love
dutiful one can be, still devoid of love.
Living close, but hearts are miles apart
Sometimes distant, but they live in your heart.

What you feel , doesn't come from a person
It originates within, the spring of emotions.
Sometimes you never can control what to feel
Love is boundless, let it flow ,
 feel it like a breeze.

Love doesn't need a label or commitment
It's a feeling that must come with no restrictions.
It's not about possession or control,

It's about letting go and letting it grow.

Love is a force that cannot be contained
It's a power that cannot be restrained.
It's a connection that transcends time and space
It's a feeling so strong, one can't erase.

So let love be free and let it soar
It will find its way to your heart's core
Don't try to control or define its direction
Just let it flow and feel its perfection.

A friend's embrace

When sorrow's cloak descends upon your heart,
I'll be your beacon, easing every part.
A listening ear, a shoulder to lean on,
Through darkest times, together we'll have
drawn.

With gentle words, I'll lift your heavy load,
Unburdening your soul with stories untold.
No judgment cast, no scorn in my gaze,
I'll guide you through this path, your steps to
raise.

Through joyous triumphs and adversity's might,
I'll be your rock, your unwavering light.
Celebrating your victories, holding you dear,
Comforting your wounds, dispelling your fear.

When words escape, a silent embrace will do,
Conveying care and love, strong and true.
Your laughter and tears, I'll hold with pride,
A faithful witness, by your side I'll abide.

Through laughter's echo and tears' gentle fall,
Our friendship's bond will never falter or stall.
In eternity's tapestry, our names entwined,

Forever connected, our spirits aligned.

For in your presence, I find solace and grace,
A true friend forever, in this earthly space.
Through sorrow's gloom or joy's radiant hue,
I'll be your companion, walking beside you.

The window with a view

To most, it was just a window
for me, it brought my visual treats
The gulmohar on trees, the smell of rain
a million memories buried underneath.

The day I spotted that peacock
I shifted my seat for the sight once more
The soothing breeze touched my cheeks
I forgot the worries, gnawing deep.

The window knew my numerous stories,
It saw my tears and countless glories.
Staring out at hills, I released my stress
For in silence it stood, when it saw me distressed

Fifteen years was a very long time
Me and the window learnt to put things behind
Now that I won't see it anymore
Know not where to seek sunshine like before
A silent companion I lost forever
who showed me a world and changed me
forever

Run dear, Run!

Run, because it is fast
before your negative thoughts catch up and hit.
Run because it is easier to do
than blend and lose your hard ground too

Roots are what hold you to dirt
It is the branch that sways and never rests.
Look for the sunshine, turn and run,
run, for that might be a sign from the sun.

Run, because the rainbow is far
Don't seek a colour that might turn grey afterall
The only hope that sun shine brings
Is the vibrant rainbow seen up hill

Run , because you can do it now
Spread your wings and the wind can guide you
now
Flow like a river, bend, but don't return
Run , don't stop, till you find heaven.

The Detachment

I sensed a sense of detachment
When the texts became scarce
and dry, devoid of emotions!
Once filled with intense feelings
Now a mere acknowledgement

When words were replaced by heart emojis
I understood the reality of being busy
But it also meant I was just an option
Among tasks that needed prioritization
I'm not sure why I still wait
to hear about your well-being

My addiction is beyond my control
I surrendered my heart a while ago
I yearn intensely to be close to you
The distance is agonizing,
I wonder if it bothers you?
My heart aches more each day
Knowing our time slipping day by day.
And I may not have the chance to see you again
When you find the time someday, may be I will
be gone by then

The loving hands

In the gentle dance of intertwined hands,
Lies a story of intimacy, that few understand.
Fingers weave a connection so fine,
Tracing veins, sensing life's design.

Heartbeats merge in a rhythmic embrace,
As love's warmth floods each open space.
Hands cradle face, tender and true,
Drowning souls in affection's gentle hue.

Down necks and shoulders, they roam,
Sending shivers to the depths of home.
For in the touch of hands, emotions unfold,
A tapestry of intimacy, precious and bold.

They refuse to hide the love they bear,
In every touch, a universe to share.
Hands, forever symbols of connection's art,
In their grasp, we find solace, never apart.

Never dim your light

That glint after every stint
the smile with a subtle hint
swaying away worries
patient, with no hurries

Your shine just outshines all!

Hold on to merry laughs
Celebrating even a fall
You dance like no one is watching
Isn't that magic eye-catching?

You are a dream in every attire
You create a path for what you desire
Your aura is what radiates through
It's magic for anyone close to you.

You bring joy wherever you go
dispelling darkness with your inner glow.
Your spirit is contagious
your energy ageless.

You are a beacon of hope
A true inspiration, a mighty force.

Guiding others with grace
you leave a lasting trace.

So keep shining bright
in your own unique light.
For you are truly one of a kind
a magical force, a rare find!

Dance my way to life

In the rhythm of life, I'll sway and twirl,
With each step, my spirit unfurls.
In the melody of dreams, I'll find my tune,
Underneath the radiant, silver moon.

I will dance my way through stormy skies,
With courage gleaming in my eyes.
Through trials and tribulations, I'll glide,
In the dance of resilience, I'll abide.

Amidst hopeful blooms, I'll elegantly spin,
Embracing every moment, within.
With fervor as my companion, I'll sway,
Fearlessly, in the dance, I'll stay.

With every beat, I'll find my grace,
In the chaos, I'll find my place.
I'll waltz through joy, I'll tango through pain,
Dancing through sunshine and through rain.

In the grand ballroom of life, I'll whirl,
Where every twist is a tale unfurl.
For in the dance of existence, I'll sway,
"I will dance my way," I proudly say.